Recipe Collection

COOKIES

Recipe Collection

COOKIES

Publications International, Ltd.

Favorite Brand Name Recipes at www.fbnr.com

Recipes developed and tested by Land O'Lakes Test Kitchens. For questions regarding recipes in this cookbook or LAND O LAKES® products, call: 1-800-328-4155.

Special thanks to the staff of Land O'Lakes, Inc., including Amy Jeatran, Publisher; Becky Wahlund, Director of Test Kitchens; Marge Ryerson, Editor; and Pat Weed, Publications Coordinator.

Pictured on the front cover: Browned Butter Cashew Shortbread Cookies (page 34).

Pictured on the back cover: Key Lime Shortbread Cookies (page 68), Best Ever Butter Cookies (page 72), Paradise Cookies (page 21).

ISBN-13: 978-1-4127-2704-4
ISBN-10: 1-4127-2704-9

Manufactured in China.

8 7 6 5 4 3 2 1

Preparation and Cooking Times: All recipes were developed and tested in the Land O'Lakes Test Kitchens by professional home economists. Use "Preparation Time" and "Cooking, Baking, Microwaving or Broiling Time" given with each recipe as guides. Preparation time is based on the approximate amount of "active" time required to assemble the recipe. This includes steps such as chopping, mixing, cooking pasta, frosting, etc. Cooking, baking, microwaving or broiling times are based on the minimum amount of time required for these recipe steps.

CONTENTS

11

54

90

75

COOKIES
It's better with butter

Nothing equals the wonderful flavor of real butter and the homemade goodness it adds to baked goods. When you bake, butter plays a major role in tenderizing, adding flavor and color, and helping your baked goods to brown. Here are some tips for better baking with butter:

What is the best way to soften butter? Soften butter for easier mixing by removing it from the refrigerator and letting it stand 30 to 45 minutes at room temperature. In a hurry? Cut butter into chunks and let stand 15 minutes at room temperature, or place a stick of cold butter between sheets of waxed paper and hit it with a rolling pin on each side to smash it. We don't recommend softening butter in the microwave because it can melt too quickly.

Can salted and unsalted butter be substituted for one another? Unsalted butter may be substituted for salted butter or vice versa. It is not necessary to alter the amount of salt in the recipe. Unsalted butter gives recipes a delicate, cultured flavor.

How long can I store my butter? Always refrigerate butter in its original wrapping, in its original package, and store in the coldest part of the refrigerator—not in the "butter keeper" in the door. Butter will retain its freshness for four months. For longer storage, place carton in a resealable plastic bag or wrap in aluminum foil and freeze.

Measuring Tips

Butter: Cut the stick at the desired marking on the wrapper, using a sharp knife.

1 cup = 2 sticks = ½ pound

⅔ cup = 10 tablespoons plus 2 teaspoons

½ cup = 1 stick = ¼ pound

⅓ cup = 5 tablespoons plus 1 teaspoon

¼ cup = ½ stick = 4 tablespoons

Flour: Stir flour with a large spoon to loosen it up. Lightly spoon flour into a dry measuring cup and level top with a spatula or knife. Do not tap or shake the measuring cup when measuring, or you will get too much flour. Sifting isn't necessary unless the recipe specifically calls for it.

Brown sugar: Pack firmly into dry measuring cup until level with top.

Cornmeal, granulated sugar, oats, and powdered sugar: Spoon into a dry measuring cup and level top with a spatula or knife.

Leavenings and spices: Fill a standard measuring spoon to the top and level with a spatula or knife.

Liquids: A common baking mistake is measuring liquid ingredients in dry measuring cups. All liquids—including milk, honey, and corn syrup—should be poured into a glass or clear plastic liquid measuring cup on a level surface. Bend down so your eye is level with the marking on the cup for an accurate reading. For easy removal of sticky liquids such as corn syrup, honey, or molasses, spray the measuring cup first with cooking spray.

For Best Results...

• Read through the entire recipe before you start to make sure you have all the necessary ingredients.

• Prepare ingredients that need to be softened, toasted, chopped, grated, or peeled first.

• Use dry measuring cups for dry ingredients and glass or clear plastic measuring cups for liquids.

The Basic Tools

The following is a list of cookie baking basics:

• Cookie and/or biscuit cutters

• Cookie sheets and baking pans

• Cooling racks

• Electric hand-held or stand-up mixer

• Kitchen timer

• Measuring cups and spoons

• Metal spatula or turner

• Mixing bowls

• Rolling pin

• Rubber spatula

• Wooden spoons

Orange & Fig Pinwheels, p. 22

Buttermint Sugar Cookies
(opposite page), p. 11

SHAPED
AND SPRITZ

Homemade means handmade for these delicious cookies. Fortunately, it also means easily made as all of these cookies are simply shaped by hand or a cookie press.

Chocolate Dipped Citrus Ribbons

Preparation time: **45 minutes** | Baking time: **7 minutes per pan** | **6½ dozen cookies**

Cookie

  1 cup LAND O LAKES® Butter, softened
 ⅔ cup sugar
  1 egg
  1 tablespoon orange juice
1½ teaspoons freshly grated orange peel
 ½ teaspoon vanilla
2½ cups all-purpose flour

Dip

1 cup white baking chips
2 tablespoons shortening
1 cup real semi-sweet chocolate chips

• Heat oven to 350°F. Combine all cookie ingredients except flour in large bowl. Beat at medium speed, scraping bowl often, until creamy. Reduce speed to low; add flour. Beat until well mixed.

• Fit cookie press with ribbon template. Fill cookie press with dough. Press long continuous strips of dough onto ungreased cookie sheet; score every 3 inches. Bake for 7 to 9 minutes or until edges are lightly browned. Cut or break apart on scored lines. Cool completely.

• Meanwhile, melt white baking chips and 1 tablespoon shortening in 1-quart saucepan over low heat, stirring occasionally, until smooth (3 to 4 minutes). Melt chocolate chips and remaining shortening in another 1-quart saucepan over low heat, stirring occasionally, until smooth (3 to 4 minutes). Pour melted mixtures side by side into a shallow dish; swirl with knife for marbled effect. Dip one end of each cookie into marbled mixture. Place cookies on cooling rack over waxed paper to set.

variations:

Lemon or Lime Ribbons: Substitute 1 tablespoon lemon or lime juice and 1½ teaspoons finely grated lemon or lime peel for orange juice and peel.

Buttermint Sugar Cookies

Preparation time: **30 minutes** | Baking time: **10 minutes per pan** | **4 dozen cookies**

  4 ounces (1 cup) soft pastel buttermints
  ½ cup sugar
  ½ cup LAND O LAKES® Butter, softened
  1 egg
  1 teaspoon vanilla
  1½ cups all-purpose flour
  1 teaspoon baking powder
  ¼ teaspoon salt
     Decorator sugar, if desired

• Heat oven to 350°F. Place buttermints and ½ cup sugar in resealable plastic food bag or between sheets of waxed paper. Crush with rolling pin or meat mallet.

• Combine mint mixture and butter in large bowl. Beat at medium speed, scraping bowl often, until creamy. Add egg and vanilla; continue beating until well mixed. Reduce speed to low; add flour, baking powder and salt. Beat until well mixed.

• Shape dough into 1-inch balls. Roll in decorator sugar, if desired. Place 2 inches apart onto ungreased cookie sheets. Bake for 10 to 12 minutes or until edges are lightly browned.

tip:
Buttermints can also be crushed in a food processor bowl fitted with metal blade.

Banana Cream Sandwich Cookies

Preparation time: **45 minutes** | Baking time: **10 minutes per pan** | **3 dozen sandwich cookies**

Cookie
- 1 cup LAND O LAKES® Butter, softened
- 1 cup sugar
- 1 medium (½ cup) ripe banana, sliced ¼-inch
- 1 egg
- 1 teaspoon vanilla
- 2⅓ cups all-purpose flour
- ¼ teaspoon salt
- ½ cup chopped pecans

Filling
- 3 cups powdered sugar
- ¼ cup LAND O LAKES® Butter, softened
- 1 teaspoon vanilla
- 2 to 3 tablespoons milk

• Heat oven to 350°F. Combine butter, sugar and banana in large bowl. Beat at low speed, scraping bowl often, until smooth. Add egg and vanilla; continue beating until well mixed. Add flour and salt; continue beating until well mixed. Stir in pecans.

• Shape dough into 1-inch balls. Place 2 inches apart onto greased cookie sheets. Flatten balls to ¼-inch thickness with buttered bottom of glass dipped in flour.

• Bake for 10 to 12 minutes or until edges are lightly browned. Remove from cookie sheets immediately; cool completely.

• Combine all filling ingredients except milk in small bowl. Beat at medium speed, gradually adding enough milk for desired spreading consistency. Spread 2 teaspoons filling on bottoms of half of cooled cookies. Top with remaining cookies, bottom-side against filling.

Almond Wreaths

Preparation time: **1 hour 30 minutes** | Baking time: **7 minutes per pan** | **5 dozen cookies**

Cookie

- 1 cup LAND O LAKES® Butter, softened
- 1 cup powdered sugar
- 1 egg
- ½ teaspoon almond extract
- ⅛ teaspoon salt
- 2½ cups all-purpose flour

Glaze

- 1½ cups powdered sugar
- 1 teaspoon almond extract
- 1 teaspoon light corn syrup
- 2 to 3 tablespoons water

Decorations

Nonpareils, decorator candies and sugars, as desired

• Combine butter and 1 cup powdered sugar in large bowl. Beat at medium speed until creamy. Add egg, almond extract and salt; continue beating until mixed. Reduce speed to low; add flour; beat until well mixed. Divide dough in half. Wrap each half in plastic food wrap. Refrigerate 30 minutes.

• Heat oven to 375°F. Shape dough, one-half at a time, (keeping remaining dough refrigerated until ready to use) into 1-inch balls. Cut each ball in half; roll each half into 4½-inch rope. Gently twist two ropes together; shape into a wreath. Place 1-inch apart onto ungreased cookie sheets. Bake for 7 to 8 minutes or until edges are lightly browned. Cool 1 minute; remove from cookie sheets. Place onto waxed paper; cool completely.

• Combine all glaze ingredients in small bowl; stir until smooth. Brush glaze onto cooled cookies using pastry brush; immediately sprinkle with decorations, as desired.

Vanilla & Chocolate Biscotti

Preparation time: **45 minutes** | Baking time: **37 minutes** | **3 dozen biscotti**

Biscotti

- 2 cups all-purpose flour
- ½ cup finely chopped walnuts, toasted
- ½ teaspoon baking powder
- ½ teaspoon baking soda
- ¼ teaspoon salt
- 1 cup sugar
- ¼ cup LAND O LAKES® Butter, softened
- 2 eggs
- 2 teaspoons vanilla
- 1 (1-ounce) square unsweetened baking chocolate, melted, cooled

Glaze

- ¼ cup real semi-sweet chocolate chips
- 2 teaspoons shortening
- ¼ cup white baking chips

• Heat oven to 350°F. Combine flour, walnuts, baking powder, baking soda and salt in small bowl. Set aside.

• Combine sugar and butter in large bowl. Beat at medium speed, scraping bowl often, until well mixed. Add eggs and vanilla; continue beating until well mixed. Reduce speed to low; add flour mixture. Beat until well mixed.

• Remove half of dough from bowl. Add melted chocolate to remaining dough in bowl. Beat at low speed until well mixed.

• Divide chocolate dough and vanilla dough into two equal portions. Roll each portion on lightly floured surface into 6-inch log. Place 1 chocolate log on top of 1 vanilla log; shape into 10×1½-inch log. Repeat with remaining dough to form second log. Place each log, 3 inches apart, onto ungreased cookie sheet. Bake for 23 to 28 minutes or until set and lightly browned. Let cool on cookie sheet 15 minutes.

• Reduce oven temperature to 300°F. Cut logs diagonally into ½-inch slices with serrated knife. Arrange slices on cookie sheet, cut-side down. Bake for 14 to 18 minutes, turning once, or until crisp and golden brown on both sides. Place on cooling racks; cool completely.

• Melt chocolate chips and 1 teaspoon shortening in 1-quart saucepan over low heat, stirring occasionally, until smooth (1 to 2 minutes). Repeat with white baking chips and remaining shortening. Drizzle glaze over biscotti.

Holiday Meringues

Preparation time: **30 minutes** | Baking time: **48 minutes** | **3½ dozen cookies**

  4 egg whites, room temperature
  2 teaspoons almond extract
  ½ teaspoon cream of tartar
  1 cup sugar
  4 drops green food color

  Red and green candied cherries, cut as desired

• Heat oven to 275°F. Combine egg whites, almond extract and cream of tartar in large bowl. Beat at medium speed, scraping bowl often, until soft peaks form (about 1 minute). Increase speed to high. Beat, gradually adding sugar 2 tablespoons at a time and scraping bowl often, until stiff peaks form and sugar is almost dissolved (2 to 3 minutes). Stir in food color.

• Place meringue in pastry bag fitted with large star tip (number 8). Pipe onto parchment-lined cookie sheets forming 2-inch wreaths; decorate with candied cherries. Bake for 25 minutes.

• Reduce oven temperature to 250°F. Continue baking for 23 to 27 minutes or until edges are set. Cool on parchment paper.

tip:
You can use cookie sheets lined with aluminum foil and sprayed with no-stick cooking spray for parchment-lined cookie sheets.

tip:
It is important to make sure no egg yolk gets into the egg whites. Egg yolk will keep the egg whites from forming stiff peaks.

Pink Lemonade Wafers

Preparation time: **40 minutes** | Baking time: **5 minutes per pan** | **4½ dozen cookies**

- 1 cup sugar
- ¼ cup LAND O LAKES® Butter, softened
- 1 egg
- 2 teaspoons freshly grated lemon peel
- 1 teaspoon lemon juice
- 1 to 2 drops red food color
- 1 cup all-purpose flour
- ½ teaspoon baking powder
- ¼ teaspoon salt

   Powdered sugar, if desired

• Heat oven to 400°F. Combine ½ cup sugar, butter, egg, lemon peel, lemon juice and red food color in large bowl. Beat at medium speed, scraping bowl often, until creamy. Reduce speed to low; add flour, baking powder and salt. Beat until well mixed. Cover; refrigerate until firm (1 hour).

• Shape dough into ½-inch balls; roll in remaining sugar. Place 2 inches apart onto ungreased cookie sheets. Flatten balls to ¼-inch thickness with bottom of buttered glass dipped in sugar. Bake for 5 to 7 minutes or until edges are lightly browned. Sprinkle with powdered sugar, if desired.

Chocolate Spritz Cookies

Preparation time: **1 hour** | Baking time: **9 minutes per pan** | **5 dozen cookies**

Cookie

- ¾ cup LAND O LAKES® Butter, softened
- ½ cup sugar
- 1 egg yolk
- 3 tablespoons milk
- 1 tablespoon vanilla
- 2 (1-ounce) squares unsweetened baking chocolate, melted, cooled
- 2 cups all-purpose flour
- ½ teaspoon salt

Glaze

- ¼ cup LAND O LAKES® Butter
- 1 cup powdered sugar
- ¾ to 1 teaspoon rum extract or vanilla
- 1 to 2 tablespoons hot water

  Decorator sugars

• Heat oven to 375°F. Combine ¾ cup butter, sugar, egg yolk, milk and vanilla in large bowl. Beat at medium speed, scraping bowl often, until creamy. Add chocolate; continue beating, scraping bowl often, until well mixed. Reduce speed to low; add flour and salt. Beat, scraping bowl often, until well mixed. (If dough is too soft, cover and refrigerate at least 30 minutes or until firm enough to form cookies.)

• Place dough in cookie press; form desired shapes 1 inch apart onto ungreased cookie sheets. Bake for 9 to 12 minutes or until set. Cool completely.

• Melt ¼ cup butter in 1-quart saucepan; stir in powdered sugar and rum extract until smooth. Gradually add enough water for desired glazing consistency. Glaze cooled cookies; sprinkle immediately with decorator sugars.

Holiday Shortbread Tidbits

Preparation time: **20 minutes** | Baking time: **14 minutes per pan** | **256 tidbits**

> ½ cup LAND O LAKES® Butter, softened
> ¼ cup sugar
> ¼ teaspoon almond extract
> 1¼ cups all-purpose flour
> ¼ teaspoon salt
> 4 teaspoons multi-colored nonpareils

• Heat oven to 325°F. Line 8-inch square baking pan with plastic food wrap, leaving 1-inch overhang. Set aside.

• Combine butter, sugar and almond extract in medium bowl. Beat at medium speed, scraping bowl often, until creamy. Reduce speed to low; add flour and salt. Beat until well mixed. Stir in nonpareils.

• Knead mixture 4 to 5 times in bowl until dough forms a ball. Pat dough evenly into prepared pan. Use plastic wrap to lift dough from pan. Cut dough into ½-inch squares. Gently place squares ½ inch apart onto ungreased cookie sheets; discard plastic wrap. Bake for 14 to 16 minutes or until bottoms just begin to brown.

tip:
Avoid last minute holiday hassle—make these sweet tidbits before the holiday season. Store between sheets of waxed paper in container with tight-fitting lid; freeze for up to 2 months.

Chocolate Hazelnut Spirals

Preparation time: **30 minutes** | Baking time: **8 minutes per pan** | **4 dozen cookies**

   2   cups all-purpose flour
   1   teaspoon baking powder
   ¼   teaspoon salt
   ¾   cup LAND O LAKES® Butter, softened
   1   cup sugar
   1   egg
 1½   teaspoons vanilla
   ¼   cup chocolate-hazelnut spread
   ¼   cup skinned hazelnuts, toasted, ground

• Combine flour, baking powder and salt in medium bowl. Set aside.

• Place butter and sugar in large bowl. Beat at medium speed, scraping bowl often, until creamy. Add egg and vanilla; continue beating until well mixed. Reduce speed to low; add flour mixture. Beat until well mixed.

• Remove 1½ cups dough. To remaining dough, add chocolate-hazelnut spread and ground hazelnuts; mix well. Divide each dough in half, making 4 portions. Shape each portion of dough into rectangle. Roll each portion between 2 sheets of waxed paper into thin 10×6-inch rectangle. Remove top sheets of waxed paper. Invert 1 chocolate rectangle on top of 1 plain dough rectangle; remove top sheet of waxed paper. Roll up tightly into log, starting at short end. Press in ends of roll to even. Wrap in waxed paper or plastic food wrap. Repeat with remaining portions of dough. Refrigerate until firm (2 hours or overnight).

• Heat oven to 375°F. Cut logs into ¼-inch slices with sharp knife. Place 1 inch apart onto ungreased cookie sheets. Bake for 8 to 11 minutes or until set and lightly browned.

Paradise Cookies

Preparation time: **45 minutes** | Baking time: **12 minutes per pan** | **3 dozen cookies**

  ¾ cup sugar
  ½ cup LAND O LAKES® Butter, softened
  1 (8-ounce) can crushed pineapple in juice, well-drained
  1 teaspoon vanilla
1¾ cups all-purpose flour
  1 teaspoon baking powder
  1 (3.25-ounce) jar (⅔ cup) macadamia nuts, chopped
  ¾ cup sweetened flaked coconut

• Heat oven to 350°F. Combine sugar and butter in large bowl. Beat at medium speed, scraping bowl often, until creamy. Add pineapple and vanilla; continue beating until well mixed. Reduce speed to low; add flour and baking powder. Beat until well mixed. Stir in nuts and ¼ cup coconut. Place remaining ½ cup coconut in small, shallow bowl.

• Shape dough into 1-inch balls; dip top of each cookie into remaining coconut. Place 2 inches apart onto ungreased cookie sheets. Bake for 12 to 15 minutes or until set. Let cool 2 minutes before removing from cookie sheets.

Orange & Fig Pinwheels

Preparation time: **1 hour** | Baking time: **6 minutes per pan** | **6 dozen cookies**

Filling

  1 (9-ounce) package dried Mission figs, chopped
¼ cup sugar
½ cup orange juice

Cookie

  1 cup LAND O LAKES® Butter, softened
¾ cup sugar
½ cup firmly packed brown sugar
  2 eggs
  1 tablespoon freshly grated orange peel
  1 teaspoon vanilla
2¾ cups all-purpose flour
½ teaspoon baking soda

- Place figs and sugar in food processor bowl fitted with metal blade. Add orange juice. Cover; process until smooth (1 to 2 minutes).

- Place fig mixture in 2-quart saucepan. Cook over medium heat, stirring constantly, until mixture is thickened (4 to 6 minutes). Remove from heat. Let stand until cool (30 to 45 minutes).

- Combine butter, sugar and brown sugar in large bowl. Beat at medium speed, scraping bowl often, until creamy. Add eggs, orange peel and vanilla; continue beating until well mixed. Reduce speed to low; add flour and baking soda. Beat until well mixed. Divide dough in half; wrap each in plastic food wrap. Refrigerate until firm (2 hours or overnight).

- Roll out dough, one-half at a time (keeping remaining dough refrigerated), on lightly floured surface to form 10×9-inch rectangle. Spread with half of cooled fig mixture, leaving ½-inch border at two long sides. Roll up tightly, starting with short side, to form 9-inch log. Wrap in plastic food wrap. Repeat with remaining dough and filling. Freeze 2 hours or overnight.

- Heat oven to 375°F. Remove 1 log from freezer. Slice into ¼-inch slices with sharp knife; place onto ungreased cookie sheets. Bake for 6 to 8 minutes or until lightly browned. Repeat with remaining log.

Caramel Praline
Walnut Bars, p. 28

Gooey Chocolate Cashew Bars
(opposite page), p. 32

CRAZY
FOR NUTS

Nuts and cookies are a delightful combination. Almonds, cashews, hazelnuts, macadamias, peanuts, pecans, pistachios, or walnuts—pick any one and add flavor, texture, and a visual aesthetic that's hard to beat.

Double Almond Pastry Bars

Preparation time: **10 minutes** | Baking time: **14 minutes** | 48 bars

   ½ (17.3-ounce) package (1 sheet) frozen puff pastry, thawed
   1 (10-ounce) can almond filling
   ½ cup sliced almonds

• Heat oven to 375°F. Roll out pastry to 15×10-inch rectangle. Place into ungreased 15×10×1-inch jelly-roll pan. Bake for 12 minutes.

• Place almond filling in small microwave-safe bowl. Microwave on HIGH until warm (about 1 minute). Stir almonds into filling. Spread evenly over hot partially baked pastry. Continue baking for 2 to 4 minutes or until topping has set.

• Cool 15 minutes; cut into bars. Serve warm or cool.

Toasted Almond Macaroon Bars

Preparation time: **15 minutes** | Baking time: **32 minutes** | **36 bars**

Crust
1¼ cups all-purpose flour
½ cup LAND O LAKES® Butter, softened
½ cup firmly packed brown sugar

Filling
3 eggs, slightly beaten
½ cup sugar
½ cup firmly packed brown sugar
¼ cup light corn syrup
¼ cup LAND O LAKES® Butter, melted
1 teaspoon vanilla
2 cups sweetened flaked coconut
¾ cup slivered almonds, chopped, toasted

Glaze
⅓ cup real semi-sweet chocolate chips
2 teaspoons shortening

• Heat oven to 350°F. Combine all crust ingredients in small bowl. Beat at low speed, scraping bowl often, until mixture resembles coarse crumbs. Press mixture evenly onto bottom of ungreased 13×9-inch baking pan. Bake for 12 to 15 minutes or until just beginning to brown.

• Meanwhile, combine all filling ingredients except coconut and almonds in large bowl; mix well. Stir in coconut and almonds. Spread evenly over hot, partially baked crust. Bake for 20 to 30 minutes or until light golden brown. Cool completely.

• Place chocolate chips and shortening in small microwave-safe bowl. Microwave on HIGH 1 minute; stir. Continue microwaving 30 seconds; stir until smooth. Drizzle over bars. Cool completely. Cut into bars.

Caramel Praline Walnut Bars

Preparation time: **25 minutes** | Baking time: **29 minutes** | **48 bars**

Crust

1¾ cups all-purpose flour

⅓ cup firmly packed brown sugar

¼ teaspoon baking powder

¾ cup LAND O LAKES® Butter

Topping

⅓ cup LAND O LAKES® Butter

1½ cups chopped walnuts

½ cup sugar

½ cup firmly packed brown sugar

½ cup light corn syrup

1 tablespoon water

1 teaspoon salt

⅓ cup LAND O LAKES™ Heavy Whipping Cream

1½ teaspoons vanilla

• Heat oven to 350°F. Line 13×9-inch baking pan with aluminum foil, extending foil over edges. Butter foil on bottom and up sides of pan.

• Combine flour, ⅓ cup brown sugar and baking powder in large bowl; cut in ¾ cup butter until mixture resembles coarse crumbs. Pat mixture onto bottom of prepared pan. Bake for 15 minutes or until edges are lightly browned.

• Melt ⅓ cup butter in 2-quart saucepan over low heat, stirring constantly (2 to 3 minutes). Stir in walnuts, sugar, ½ cup brown sugar, corn syrup, water and salt. Increase heat to medium. Cook, stirring occasionally, until mixture comes to a boil (4 to 5 minutes). Continue boiling until candy thermometer reaches 248°F (4 to 6 minutes). Stir in whipping cream and vanilla.

• Pour filling mixture over hot, partially baked crust. Bake for 14 to 16 minutes or until mixture bubbles over entire surface. Cool completely. Lift out of pan, using foil. Cut into bars.

tip:

Pralines are a rich candy made with sugar, cream, butter and nuts. Walnuts toast in the boiling sugar-butter mixture before topping a rich shortbread crust. Be sure to cut the bars small, because they're very rich!

crazy for nuts

Pecan Glazed Butter Crescents

Preparation time: **25 minutes** | Baking time: **11 minutes per pan** | **5 dozen cookies**

Cookie

- 1 cup LAND O LAKES® Butter, softened
- ⅔ cup sugar
- 2 teaspoons vanilla
- 2 cups all-purpose flour
- 1 cup pecans, toasted, ground
- ¼ teaspoon salt

Glaze

- 1½ cups powdered sugar
- 3 to 4 tablespoons bourbon or water

Finely chopped pecans, if desired

• Heat oven to 350°F. Combine butter, sugar and vanilla in large bowl. Beat at medium speed, scraping bowl often, until creamy. Reduce speed to low; add all remaining cookie ingredients. Beat until well mixed.

• Shape dough into 1-inch balls; form into crescents. Place 1 inch apart onto ungreased cookie sheets. Bake for 11 to 14 minutes or until set. Cool completely.

• Combine powdered sugar and enough bourbon in small bowl for thin glazing consistency. Drizzle cooled cookies with glaze. Immediately sprinkle with finely chopped pecans, if desired.

tip:

To shape into a crescent, roll the ball of dough between your palms. Form a short log with tapered ends and curve slightly into a crescent shape.

Chewy Chocolate
Chunk Bars, p. 48

Latte Bars
(opposite page), p. 54

BROWNIES & BARS

Brownies and bars offer the incomparable taste of homemade cookies without any fuss or bother. Simply mix the batter, spread in a pan, and bake.

Cranberry Vanilla Chip Bars

Preparation time: **15 minutes** | Baking time: **25 minutes** | **16 bars**

Bar

½ cup sugar

⅓ cup LAND O LAKES® Butter, softened

¼ cup firmly packed brown sugar

1 egg

1 teaspoon vanilla

1 cup all-purpose flour

½ teaspoon baking powder

¼ teaspoon salt

½ cup sweetened dried cranberries

½ cup white baking chips

½ cup chopped pecans, if desired

Glaze

¼ cup white baking chips

½ teaspoon shortening

• Heat oven to 350°F. Grease and flour 8-inch square baking pan. Set aside.

• Combine sugar, butter, brown sugar, egg and vanilla in large bowl. Beat at medium speed, scraping bowl often, until well mixed. Reduce speed to low; add flour, baking powder and salt. Beat until well mixed. Stir in cranberries, ½ cup white baking chips and pecans.

• Spread batter into prepared pan. Bake for 25 to 30 minutes or until toothpick inserted in center comes out clean. Cool completely.

• Melt ¼ cup white baking chips and shortening in 1-quart saucepan over low heat, stirring constantly, until smooth. Drizzle over cooled bars. Cut into bars.

Sugarplum Bars

Preparation time: **20 minutes** | Baking time: **45 minutes** | 25 bars

Crust

1⅓ cups all-purpose flour
½ cup powdered sugar
⅛ teaspoon salt
½ cup cold LAND O LAKES® Butter

Topping

¾ cup sugar
15 dried plums
2 teaspoons cornstarch
½ teaspoon baking powder
⅛ teaspoon salt
1 egg
2 tablespoons lemon juice

1 tablespoon purple coarse sparkling or sanding sugar

• Heat oven to 350°F. Line bottom and sides of 8-inch square baking pan with aluminum foil; extending foil beyond ends. Grease foil.

• Combine all crust ingredients except butter in medium bowl; cut in butter with pastry blender or fork until mixture resembles coarse crumbs. Reserve ¾ cup mixture. Pat remaining mixture onto bottom of prepared pan. Bake for 15 minutes.

• Meanwhile, place sugar, dried plums, cornstarch, baking powder and ⅛ teaspoon salt in processor bowl fitted with metal blade. Cover; pulse until dried plums are finely ground. Add egg and lemon juice; continue processing 20 seconds to combine.

• Pour plum mixture over hot, partially baked crust; sprinkle with reserved crust mixture and coarse sugar. Continue baking for 30 to 35 minutes or until edges are browned and topping is set. Cool completely. Lift bars out by overhanging foil and cut into bars.

tip:

The fruit in this bar is dried plums, a new name for an old product, prunes. In French, *prune* means plum so both names are accurate. The best dried plums are still moist. If stored a bit too long, soak them briefly in hot water and then drain.

Strawberry Meringue Bars

Preparation time: **15 minutes** | Baking time: **37 minutes** | **36 bars**

Crust

   2 cups all-purpose flour
   ½ cup sugar
   ½ cup cold LAND O LAKES® Butter
   3 egg yolks

Topping

   3 egg whites
   ¼ teaspoon cream of tartar
   1 cup powdered sugar
   ½ cup strawberry preserves
   ¼ cup sliced almonds

• Heat oven to 350°F. Combine flour and ½ cup sugar in medium bowl; cut in butter with pastry blender or fork until mixture resembles coarse crumbs. Stir in egg yolks until well mixed. Press onto bottom of ungreased 13×9-inch baking pan. Bake for 15 to 20 minutes or until edges are lightly browned.

• Meanwhile, beat egg whites and cream of tartar in small bowl at high speed until foamy (45 to 60 seconds). Continue beating, gradually adding powdered sugar, until glossy and stiff peaks form (1 to 1½ minutes).

• Spread preserves over hot, partially baked crust. Spread egg white mixture over preserves; sprinkle with almonds. Continue baking for 22 to 27 minutes or until light golden brown. Cool completely. Cut into bars with sharp, wet knife.

Easy Saucepan Brownies

Preparation time: **15 minutes** | Baking time: **14 minutes** | **48 brownies**

Brownie
- 1 cup LAND O LAKES® Butter
- 4 (1-ounce) squares unsweetened baking chocolate
- 2 cups sugar
- 1½ cups all-purpose flour
- 4 eggs

Frosting
- 1 cup real semi-sweet chocolate chips
- 2 tablespoons shortening
- 1½ cups powdered sugar
- ½ teaspoon vanilla
- 3 to 5 tablespoons milk

• Heat oven to 350°F. Combine butter and chocolate in 3-quart saucepan. Cook over medium heat, stirring constantly, until melted (3 to 5 minutes). Stir in all remaining brownie ingredients until well mixed.

• Spread into greased 15×10×1-inch jelly-roll pan. Bake for 14 to 16 minutes or until brownies just begin to pull away from sides of pan. Cool completely.

• Melt chocolate chips and shortening in 1-quart saucepan over low heat, stirring occasionally, until smooth (3 to 5 minutes). Stir in powdered sugar, ½ teaspoon vanilla and enough milk for desired spreading consistency. Spread over cooled brownies. Cut into bars.

No-Bake Rocky Road Chocolate Bars

Preparation time: **20 minutes** | **48 bars**

- ½ cup LAND O LAKES® Butter
- 1 (12-ounce) package (2 cups) real semi-sweet chocolate chips
- 1 cup butterscotch-flavored chips
- 1 cup peanut butter
- 4 cups crisp rice cereal
- 3 cups miniature marshmallows

• Combine butter, chocolate chips and butterscotch chips in 4-quart saucepan. Cook over low heat, stirring constantly, until melted (4 to 6 minutes). Stir in peanut butter until well mixed.

• Remove from heat. Add cereal and marshmallows; toss until well coated.

• Press mixture onto bottom of buttered 13×9-inch baking pan. Refrigerate until firm (about 30 minutes).

• Cut into bars. Store refrigerated.

Browned Butter Frosted Pumpkin Bars

Preparation time: **20 minutes** | Baking time: **20 minutes** | **60 bars**

Bar

1½ cups all-purpose flour

1¼ cups sugar

2 teaspoons baking powder

2 teaspoons ground cinnamon

1 teaspoon baking soda

½ teaspoon ground ginger

¾ cup LAND O LAKES® Butter, melted

1 (15-ounce) can pumpkin

3 eggs

¾ cup chopped sweetened dried cranberries

Frosting

½ cup LAND O LAKES® Butter

4 cups powdered sugar

1 teaspoon vanilla

¼ to ⅓ cup milk

• Heat oven to 350°F. Combine flour, sugar, baking powder, cinnamon, baking soda and ginger in large bowl. Stir in ¾ cup butter, pumpkin and eggs; mix well. Stir in cranberries.

• Spread batter into ungreased 15×10×1-inch jelly-roll pan. Bake for 20 to 25 minutes or until toothpick inserted in center comes out clean. Cool completely.

• Meanwhile, melt ½ cup butter in 1-quart saucepan over medium heat, stirring constantly and watching closely, until butter just starts to turn golden brown (3 to 5 minutes). (Butter will get foamy and bubble.) Immediately remove from heat. Pour into medium bowl; cool 5 minutes.

• Add powdered sugar and vanilla to cooled browned butter; mix well. Stir in enough milk for desired frosting consistency. Spread frosting over cooled bars. Cut into bars.

Chewy Chocolate Chunk Bars

Preparation time: **15 minutes** | Baking time: **24 minutes** | 48 bars

Bar

- 2 cups firmly packed brown sugar
- 1½ cups LAND O LAKES® Butter, softened
- 2 eggs
- 2 teaspoons vanilla
- ¼ teaspoon almond extract
- 3 cups uncooked old-fashioned or quick-cooking oats
- 2 cups all-purpose flour
- ½ teaspoon baking soda
- 8 (1-ounce) squares semi-sweet or bittersweet baking chocolate, chopped
- ½ cup chopped pecans or walnuts

Glaze

- 1 (1-ounce) square semi-sweet or bittersweet baking chocolate
- ½ teaspoon shortening
- 1 (1-ounce) square white baking chocolate
- ½ teaspoon shortening

• Heat oven to 350°F. Combine brown sugar and butter in large bowl. Beat at medium speed, scraping bowl often, until creamy. Add eggs, vanilla and almond extract; continue beating until well mixed. Reduce speed to low; add oats, flour and baking soda. Beat until well mixed. Stir in 8 ounces chopped chocolate and pecans.

• Spread batter into ungreased 15×10×1-inch jelly-roll pan. Bake for 24 to 27 minutes or until set. Cool completely.

• Place 1 square semi-sweet chocolate and ½ teaspoon shortening in small microwave-safe bowl. Microwave on MEDIUM (50% power), stirring occasionally, until melted (1 to 1½ minutes). Drizzle over cooled bars. Repeat with white chocolate and remaining shortening. Cool completely until chocolate is set. Cut into bars.

White Chocolate Cherry Shortbread

Preparation time: **20 minutes** | Baking time: **22 minutes** | **32 wedges**

Shortbread
- 1 cup LAND O LAKES® Butter, softened
- ½ cup sugar
- 1 teaspoon vanilla
- 2⅓ cups all-purpose flour
- 1 cup dried cherries, chopped
- ¾ cup white baking chips

Drizzle
- ½ cup white baking chips
- 2 teaspoons shortening

• Heat oven to 350°F. Combine butter, sugar and vanilla in large bowl. Beat at medium speed, scraping bowl often, until creamy. Reduce speed to low; add flour. Beat until mixture resembles course crumbs. Stir in cherries and white baking chips.

• Press mixture firmly and evenly into 2 ungreased 9-inch round baking pans. Bake for 22 to 26 minutes or until edges are light golden brown. Cool 15 minutes. Immediately cut each pan into 16 wedges. Cool completely. Remove from pans.

• Melt white chocolate and shortening in 1-quart saucepan over low heat, stirring occasionally, until smooth. Drizzle over cooled wedges. Let stand until set.

tip:
Shortbread has a drier and more crumbly dough, so make sure to press it firmly into each pan before baking to ensure the dough holds together.

PB & Jam Bites

Preparation time: **20 minutes** | **32 bars**

Bar
3 cups miniature marshmallows
1 cup crunchy peanut butter
½ cup LAND O LAKES® Butter
4½ cups crisp rice cereal

Filling
⅔ cup strawberry, apricot or peach jam

Topping
½ cup milk chocolate chips
1 tablespoon crunchy peanut butter
2 teaspoons shortening

• Melt marshmallows, 1 cup peanut butter and butter in 3-quart saucepan over low heat, stirring constantly, until smooth (4 to 5 minutes). Add cereal; quickly stir until well coated. Press mixture into ungreased 11×7-inch pan.

• Spoon jam by teaspoonfuls over hot cereal mixture; gently spread over top.

• Melt chocolate chips, 1 tablespoon peanut butter and shortening in 1-quart saucepan over low heat, stirring occasionally, until smooth (2 to 4 minutes). Gently spread over jam layer. Refrigerate until chocolate layer is firm (about 2 hours). Cut into bars.

tip:
One of the world's great convenience foods, peanut butter, was first developed in 1890 and promoted at the St. Louis World's Fair in 1904. It's made from ground peanuts, vegetable oil and salt. Sometimes sugar and additives are added to make it creamier or to prevent the oil from separating. Natural peanut butter should be refrigerated after opening. Most other peanut butters keep for up to 6 months at room temperature.

Latte Bars

Preparation time: **30 minutes** | Baking time: **23 minutes** | **25 bars**

Bar

2 to 3 teaspoons instant espresso powder*
2 teaspoons hot water
1 cup sugar
¾ cup all-purpose flour
⅓ cup unsweetened cocoa
¼ teaspoon salt
½ cup LAND O LAKES® Butter, melted
2 eggs
1 teaspoon vanilla

Frosting

½ teaspoon instant espresso powder*
1 tablespoon milk
1 cup powdered sugar
2 tablespoons LAND O LAKES® Butter, softened

1 to 2 tablespoons finely chopped chocolate-covered espresso roasted coffee beans

• Heat oven to 350°F. Combine 2 to 3 teaspoons espresso powder and hot water in small bowl; stir until dissolved. Set aside.

• Combine sugar, flour, cocoa and salt in medium bowl. Stir in ½ cup melted butter, eggs, vanilla and dissolved espresso mixture; mix well.

• Spread batter into greased 8-inch square baking pan. Bake for 23 to 28 minutes or until toothpick inserted in center comes out clean.

• Combine ½ teaspoon espresso powder and 1 tablespoon milk in small bowl; stir until dissolved. Add powdered sugar and 2 tablespoons butter. Beat at low speed, scraping bowl often, adding enough additional milk for desired spreading consistency. Frost cooled bars. Sprinkle with chopped espresso beans.

*Substitute instant coffee granules.

Spumoni
Slices, p. 60

Easy Gingerbread
Cut-Outs
(opposite page), p. 62

SLICES &
CUT-OUTS

When it comes to baking cookies, sliced cookies and cut-outs are among the recipes that can honestly be called true classics. Their classic good looks are complemented by their incredible taste and the ease with which many of the recipes can be made.

Slice & Bake Peppermint Cookies

Preparation time: **40 minutes** | Baking time: **9 minutes per pan** | **11 dozen cookies**

- 1 cup LAND O LAKES® Butter, softened
- 1 cup sugar
- 1 egg
- 1 teaspoon peppermint extract
- 2⅓ cups all-purpose flour
- ¼ teaspoon baking powder
- 3 drops red food color
- 3 drops green food color

• Combine butter and sugar in large bowl. Beat at medium speed, scraping bowl often, until creamy. Add egg and peppermint extract. Continue beating until well mixed. Reduce speed to low; add flour and baking powder. Beat until well mixed.

• Divide dough into thirds. Add red food color to one-third. Add green food color to another third. Stir each until well mixed. Leave remaining dough white. Wrap each dough in plastic food wrap; refrigerate until firm (at least 1 hour).

• Divide each color of dough into thirds. Shape each third into 12×½-inch rope on waxed paper. Gently press together 1 pink and 1 green rope. Add 1 white rope; gently press to form clover leaf-shaped multicolored roll. Repeat with remaining dough. Wrap each multicolored roll in plastic food wrap; refrigerate until firm (at least 2 hours or overnight).

• Heat oven to 350°F. Cut rolls into ¼-inch slices. Place 1 inch apart onto ungreased cookie sheets. Bake for 9 to 12 minutes or until edges are very lightly browned.

Mom's Butter Cookies

Preparation time: **45 minutes** | Baking time: **8 minutes per pan** | **3 dozen cookies**

    1 cup LAND O LAKES® Butter, softened
    ½ cup firmly packed brown sugar
    ¼ cup sugar
    2 cups all-purpose flour

• Combine all ingredients except flour in large bowl. Beat at medium speed until creamy. Reduce speed to low; add flour. Beat until well mixed.

• Divide dough in half. Wrap each half in plastic food wrap; flatten slightly. Refrigerate until firm (30 minutes or overnight).

• Heat oven to 350°F. Roll out dough on lightly floured surface, one-half at a time (keeping remaining dough refrigerated), to ⅛-inch thickness. Cut with 3-inch cookie cutters. Place 1 inch apart onto ungreased cookie sheets. Bake for 8 to 10 minutes or until edges are very lightly browned. Cool 1 minute; remove from cookie sheet.

Spumoni Slices

Preparation time: **1 hour 15 minutes** | Baking time: **9 minutes per pan** | **7 dozen cookies**

- 1 cup LAND O LAKES® Butter, softened
- 1 cup sugar
- 1 egg
- 1 teaspoon vanilla
- 2½ cups all-purpose flour
- ¼ teaspoon baking powder
- ¼ teaspoon salt
- ¼ cup finely chopped maraschino cherries, well-drained
- 2 to 3 drops red food color
- ¼ cup finely chopped pistachio nuts
- 2 to 3 drops green food color

  Ice cream, if desired
  Chopped pistachio nuts, if desired
  Stemmed maraschino cherries, if desired

• Combine butter, sugar, egg and vanilla in large bowl. Beat at medium speed, scraping bowl often, until creamy. Reduce speed to low; add flour, baking powder and salt. Beat until well mixed.

• Divide dough into thirds. Add chopped cherries and desired amount red food color to one-third; mix well by hand. Add pistachios and desired amount green food color to second third of dough; mix well by hand.

• Shape each third of dough between two sheets of lightly floured waxed paper into 7×6-inch rectangle. Layer pink, white and green dough on large sheet of plastic food wrap; press down gently. Wrap securely in plastic food wrap. Refrigerate until firm (2 hours or overnight).

• Heat oven to 350°F. Cut rectangle lengthwise into three 7×2-inch pieces with sharp knife. Cut each piece crosswise into ¼-inch slices. Place slices 1 inch apart onto ungreased cookie sheets. Bake for 9 to 11 minutes or until edges just begin to brown. Cool completely.

• Serve cookies with ice cream, chopped pistachios and maraschino cherries, if desired.

tip:
Wear plastic gloves when kneading food color into dough to prevent your hands from becoming discolored.

Easy Gingerbread Cut-Outs

Preparation time: **35 minutes** | Baking time: **7 minutes per pan** | **2 dozen cookies**

Cookie

- 1 (18.25-ounce) package spice cake mix*
- ¾ cup LAND O LAKES® Butter, softened
- 1 egg
- 2 tablespoons orange juice**
- 1 teaspoon ground cinnamon
- 1 teaspoon vanilla
- ½ teaspoon ground ginger

Frosting

- 4½ cups powdered sugar
- ⅓ cup LAND O LAKES® Butter, softened
- 2 tablespoons orange juice**
- 2 to 3 tablespoons milk
- Food color, if desired

• Combine half of cake mix and all remaining cookie ingredients in large bowl. Beat at low speed, scraping bowl often, until well mixed. Add remaining cake mix; continue beating until well mixed. Divide dough in half; wrap each in plastic food wrap. Refrigerate until firm (at least 2 hours or overnight).

• Heat oven to 375°F. Roll out dough on lightly floured surface, one-half at a time (keeping remaining dough refrigerated), to ⅛-inch thickness. Cut with 3- to 4-inch cookie cutter. Place 2 inches apart onto ungreased cookie sheets. Bake for 7 to 9 minutes or until set. Let stand 1 minute; remove from cookie sheets. Cool completely.

• Combine all frosting ingredients except milk and food color in large bowl. Beat at low speed, scraping bowl often and gradually adding enough milk for desired spreading consistency. Tint with food color, if desired. Frost cooled cookies. Decorate, as desired.

*Substitute 1 (18.25-ounce) package carrot cake mix.

**Substitute 2 tablespoons milk.

Butter Rum Sandwich Triangles

Preparation time: **35 minutes** | Baking time: **9 minutes per pan** | **3 dozen sandwich cookies**

Cookie

- ½ cup powdered sugar
- ⅓ cup finely chopped pecans
- 1 cup LAND O LAKES® Butter, softened
- 2 tablespoons light rum or milk
- ½ teaspoon vanilla
- 2 cups all-purpose flour
- ½ teaspoon baking powder
- ¼ teaspoon salt
- 3 tablespoons large grain sugar

Filling

- 1⅓ cups powdered sugar
- ¼ cup LAND O LAKES® Butter, softened
- 1½ teaspoons light rum*
- 1 to 2 tablespoons LAND O LAKES™ Half & Half or milk

• Combine ½ cup powdered sugar and pecan pieces in food processor bowl fitted with metal blade. Cover; process until pecans are very finely chopped (45 to 60 seconds). Combine sugar mixture, 1 cup butter, 2 tablespoons rum and vanilla in large bowl. Beat at medium speed, scraping bowl often, until creamy (2 to 3 minutes). Reduce speed to low; add flour, baking powder and salt. Beat until well mixed (1 to 2 minutes).

• Divide dough in half; shape each half on lightly floured surface into 10-inch-long roll. Flatten sides to form triangle on waxed paper. (Use waxed paper to help shape triangle.) Wrap each half in plastic food wrap. Refrigerate until firm (2 hours).

• Heat oven to 375°F. Cut each log into ¼-inch slices with sharp knife. Place 1 inch apart onto ungreased cookie sheets. Sprinkle triangles with large grain sugar. Bake for 9 to 11 minutes or until edges begin to brown. Cool completely.

• Meanwhile, combine all filling ingredients except half & half in small bowl. Beat at low speed, adding enough half & half for desired spreading consistency. For each sandwich cookie, spread ¾ teaspoon filling on bottom of cookie. Top with second cookie, sugar-side up. Press together gently.

*Substitute ¼ teaspoon rum extract.

tip:
Use 2 rulers to shape triangle by pushing sides flat with rulers on opposite sides at the same time.

tip:
Large grain sugar adds a sweet sparkle to the tops of cookies. If you can't find it at your supermarket, check baking specialty stores or stores that sell cake decorating supplies.

Cherry Rum Ribbons

Preparation time: **45 minutes** | Baking time: **8 minutes per pan** | **6 dozen cookies**

   1 cup LAND O LAKES® Butter, softened
   1 cup sugar
   1 egg
   2 tablespoons orange juice or water
   1 teaspoon rum flavoring
   ⅛ teaspoon salt
   3 cups all-purpose flour
   ½ teaspoon baking soda
   ½ cup dried cherries, chopped
   3 drops red food color

   ½ cup coarse sugar

• Combine butter and 1 cup sugar in large bowl; beat at medium speed until creamy. Add egg, orange juice, rum flavoring and salt. Continue beating until well mixed. Reduce speed to low; add flour and baking soda. Beat until well mixed.

• Remove half of dough from bowl. Add cherries and food color to remaining dough in bowl. Beat at low speed until just blended. Divide each dough in half again.

• Line bottom and sides of 9×5-inch loaf pan with waxed paper or plastic food wrap. Press half of cherry dough evenly onto bottom of pan. Top with half of white dough. Repeat with remaining cherry and white dough, pressing each layer firmly and evenly over last layer. Cover with waxed paper or plastic food wrap; refrigerate until firm (at least 1 hour).

• Heat oven to 375°F. Invert pan to remove dough. Peel off waxed paper. Place layered dough onto cutting surface. Cut loaf crosswise into ⅛-inch slices using sharp knife. Cut each slice in half crosswise. Place 2-inches apart onto ungreased cookie sheets. Sprinkle with sugar.

• Bake for 8 to 9 minutes or until edges are firm and bottoms are lightly browned. Cool 1 minute; remove from cookie sheets.

variation:
Chocolate Cherry Ribbons: Melt ⅓ cup real semi-sweet chocolate chips over low heat; cool. Mix into white dough. Continue as directed.

tip:
Dried cherries are available in the baking section near the dried fruit in the supermarket. Substitute sweetened dried cranberries if cherries are not available.

tip:
These cookies are perfect for freezing. Place between sheets of waxed paper in container with tight-fitting lid.

Key Lime Shortbread Cookies

Preparation time: **20 minutes** | Baking time: **9 minutes per pan** | **80 cookies**

Cookie

  1½ cups all-purpose flour
  ½ cup powdered sugar
  ½ cup cornstarch
  1 cup LAND O LAKES® Butter, softened
  1 tablespoon fresh Key lime juice
  2 teaspoons freshly grated Key lime peel

Glaze   *Half recipe*

  1¼ cups powdered sugar
  1 teaspoon freshly grated Key lime peel
  2 to 3 tablespoons fresh Key lime juice

  Freshly grated Key lime peel, if desired

• Combine flour, powdered sugar and cornstarch in medium bowl. Set aside.

• Beat butter in large bowl at medium speed until creamy. Reduce speed to low; add flour mixture and all remaining cookie ingredients. Beat until dough forms.

• Shape dough into two (10-inch) logs on lightly floured surface. Wrap each in plastic food wrap; refrigerate until firm (2 hours).

• Heat oven to 350°F. Reshape logs, if necessary. Cut into ¼-inch slices with sharp knife. Place 1 inch apart onto ungreased cookie sheets. Bake for 9 to 11 minutes or until edges are lightly browned. Cool 1 minute; remove from cookie sheets. Cool completely.

• Meanwhile, place powdered sugar and 1 teaspoon lime peel in small bowl. Gradually stir in enough lime juice for desired glazing consistency. Spoon or brush glaze on top of cookies. Let stand until glaze is hardened (15 minutes).

Soft Sugar Cookies

Preparation time: **30 minutes** | Baking time: **6 minutes per pan** | **3 dozen cookies**

1½ cups sugar

1 cup LAND O LAKES® Butter, softened

2 eggs

2 teaspoons freshly grated orange peel

1 teaspoon vanilla

4⅓ cups all-purpose flour

1 teaspoon baking powder

1 teaspoon baking soda

½ teaspoon salt

1 cup LAND O LAKES™ Sour Cream

Decorator sugars, as desired

• Combine sugar, butter, eggs, orange peel and vanilla in large bowl. Beat at medium speed, scraping bowl often, until creamy. Reduce speed to low; add flour, baking powder, baking soda and salt alternately with sour cream until well mixed.

• Divide dough into thirds; wrap each in plastic food wrap. Refrigerate until firm (at least 2 hours).

• Heat oven to 400°F. Roll out dough on lightly floured surface, one-third at a time (keeping remaining dough refrigerated), to ¼-inch thickness. Cut with 3-inch cookie cutters. Place 1 inch apart onto ungreased cookie sheets. Sprinkle with decorator sugars, as desired. Bake for 6 to 9 minutes or until edges are lightly browned.

tip:

Store cookies in a container with a tight-fitting lid to keep them soft.

Best Ever Butter Cookies

Preparation time: **40 minutes** | Baking time: **6 minutes per pan** | **3 dozen cookies**

Cookie

- 1 cup LAND O LAKES® Butter, softened
- 1 cup sugar
- 1 egg
- 2 tablespoons orange juice
- 1 tablespoon vanilla
- 2½ cups all-purpose flour
- 1 teaspoon baking powder

Frosting

- 3 cups powdered sugar
- ⅓ cup LAND O LAKES® Butter, softened
- 1 teaspoon vanilla
- 1 to 2 tablespoons milk
  Food color, if desired

  Decorator candies and/or sugars, if desired

• Combine 1 cup butter, sugar and egg in large bowl. Beat at medium speed, scraping bowl often, until creamy. Add orange juice and 1 tablespoon vanilla; mix well. Reduce speed to low; add flour and baking powder. Beat until well mixed.

• Divide dough into thirds; wrap each in plastic food wrap. Refrigerate until firm (2 to 3 hours).

• Heat oven to 400°F. Roll out dough on lightly floured surface, one-third at a time (keeping remaining dough refrigerated), to ⅛ to ¼-inch thickness. Cut with 3-inch cookie cutters. Place 1 inch apart onto ungreased cookie sheets. Bake for 6 to 10 minutes or until edges are lightly browned. Cool completely.

• Combine powdered sugar, ⅓ cup butter and 1 teaspoon vanilla in small bowl. Beat at low speed, scraping bowl often and adding enough milk for desired spreading consistency. Tint frosting with food color, if desired. Frost and decorate cooled cookies as desired.

Oatmeal Crispies

Preparation time: **20 minutes** | Baking time: **12 minutes per pan** | **4 dozen cookies**

1	cup firmly packed brown sugar
½	cup LAND O LAKES® Butter, softened
½	cup shortening
2	eggs
1	teaspoon vanilla
2	cups uncooked quick-cooking oats
1½	cups all-purpose flour
1	teaspoon baking soda
¼	teaspoon salt

• Combine brown sugar, butter and shortening in large bowl. Beat at medium speed, scraping bowl often, until creamy. Add eggs and vanilla; continue beating until well mixed. Reduce speed to low; add oats, flour, baking soda and salt. Beat, scraping bowl often, until well mixed.

• Divide dough in half. Shape each half into 6-inch log. Wrap each in plastic food wrap. Refrigerate until firm (2 to 3 hours).

• Heat oven to 350°F. Cut logs into ¼-inch slices with sharp knife. Place slices 1 inch apart onto ungreased cookie sheets. Bake for 12 to 15 minutes or until lightly browned. Let stand 1 to 2 minutes; remove from cookie sheets.

tip:

Add 1 cup raisins to dough before shaping into logs.

Orange Cranberry Slices

Preparation time: **35 minutes** | Baking time: **8 minutes** | **7½ dozen cookies**

- 1 cup LAND O LAKES® Butter, softened
- 1 cup sugar
- 1 egg
- 2 tablespoons milk
- 1 teaspoon vanilla
- 3 cups all-purpose flour
- 1½ teaspoons baking powder
- ⅔ cup chopped sweetened dried cranberries
- ¼ cup chopped pecans
- 8 to 10 drops red food color
- 2 teaspoons freshly grated orange peel

• Combine butter and sugar in large bowl. Beat at medium speed, scraping bowl often, until creamy. Add egg, milk and vanilla; continue beating until well mixed. Reduce speed to low; add flour and baking powder. Beat until mixture forms a dough.

• Remove one-third of dough. Set aside. Add dried cranberries, pecans and red food color to dough in bowl. Beat until well mixed. Knead orange peel into reserved one-third of dough.

• Line 8×4-inch loaf pan with plastic food wrap, extending wrap over ends. Divide cranberry dough in half; evenly press half of cranberry dough into pan. Evenly press orange dough on top of cranberry dough. Cover with remaining cranberry dough, pressing evenly. Overlap plastic food wrap to cover dough tightly. Refrigerate until firm (4 hours or overnight).

• Heat oven to 375°F. Remove dough from pan; unwrap. Cut dough into ¼-inch slices; cut each slice into thirds. Place 2 inches apart onto ungreased cookie sheets. Bake for 8 to 10 minutes or until edges are lightly browned.

Chocolate Peanut
Butter Shortbread, p. 88

Chocolate Glazed
Mocha Wedges
(opposite page), p. 86

MAKE MINE
CHOCOLATE

This chapter is chock full of chocolate cookies and bars. We've included easy, simple-to-make treats as well as more elaborate ones just right for a party tray.

Candy Bar Squares

Preparation time: **15 minutes** | Baking time: **28 minutes** | 48 bars

Crust
1½ cups graham cracker crumbs
⅓ cup powdered sugar
⅓ cup LAND O LAKES® Butter, melted

Filling
2 cups sweetened flaked coconut
1 (14-ounce) can sweetened condensed milk
6 (1.45-ounce) chocolate candy bars with almonds*

• Heat oven to 350°F. Combine all crust ingredients in medium bowl. Press onto bottom of ungreased 13×9-inch baking pan. Bake for 10 minutes or until edges are very lightly browned.

• Meanwhile, combine coconut and sweetened condensed milk in medium bowl. Pour over hot, partially baked crust. Continue baking for 15 to 20 minutes or until edges are lightly browned and center is set.

• Place candy bars on top of baked filling to cover entire surface. Continue baking for 3 to 4 minutes or until chocolate is melted. Spread chocolate over bars. Cool completely until chocolate is set. Cut into squares.

*Substitute 1 cup milk chocolate chips.

Chocolate Amaretto Balls

Preparation time: **25 minutes** | **3 dozen**

12 (5×2½-inch) (2 cups) finely crushed chocolate graham crackers
 1 cup powdered sugar
½ cup finely chopped almonds
¼ cup LAND O LAKES® Butter, melted
¼ cup amaretto*

   Decorator sugars or powdered sugar

• Combine all ingredients except decorator sugars in large bowl until well mixed. Shape mixture into 1-inch balls; roll in decorator sugars.

• Place onto waxed paper-lined baking sheet. Cover; refrigerate 1 hour. Store refrigerated in covered container.

*Substitute 1 tablespoon almond extract and 3 tablespoons water.

tip:
Roll again in additional sugar before serving, if desired.

Chocolate Topped Pecan Lace Cookies

Preparation time: **30 minutes** | Baking time: **7 minutes per pan** | **2 dozen cookies**

- ½ cup all-purpose flour
- ½ cup firmly packed brown sugar
- ½ cup uncooked old-fashioned oats
- ½ cup pecans, toasted, ground
- 1½ teaspoons freshly grated orange peel
- ¼ teaspoon baking powder
- 6 tablespoons LAND O LAKES® Butter, melted
- 2 tablespoons light corn syrup
- 2 tablespoons LAND O LAKES™ Heavy Whipping Cream

- 1 cup real semi-sweet chocolate chips, melted

• Heat oven to 325°F. Line cookie sheets with parchment paper. Set aside.

• Combine flour, brown sugar, oats, pecans, orange peel and baking powder in medium bowl. Combine melted butter, corn syrup and whipping cream in small bowl. Stir butter mixture into flour mixture; mix well.

• Drop dough by rounded teaspoonfuls, 4 inches apart, onto prepared cookie sheets. Bake for 7 to 8 minutes or until edges are golden brown and bubbly. Cool completely on parchment paper.

• Spread flat-side of each cookie with melted chocolate using a pastry brush or spatula. Place onto clean parchment paper or waxed paper, chocolate-side up. Let stand until chocolate has set.

tip:
Use a food processor or mini chopper to grind nuts.

Chocolate Chip Toffee Diamonds

Preparation time: **15 minutes** | Baking time: **20 minutes** | **36 bars**

  1¾ cups all-purpose flour
   ¾ cup LAND O LAKES® Butter, softened
   ½ cup firmly packed brown sugar
   1 egg
   1 teaspoon vanilla
   1 (12-ounce) package (2 cups) real semi-sweet chocolate chips
   ½ cup coarsely chopped pecans

• Heat oven to 350°F. Combine all ingredients except chocolate chips and pecans in large bowl. Beat at medium speed, scraping bowl often, until well mixed. Stir in 1 cup chocolate chips.

• Spread batter into ungreased 13×9-inch baking pan. Bake for 20 to 30 minutes or until golden brown. Immediately sprinkle with remaining chocolate chips. Allow chocolate to melt slightly (2 to 3 minutes). Spread chocolate over bars; sprinkle with pecans. Cool completely. Cut into diamond-shaped bars.

Filled Sandwich Creams

Preparation time: **30 minutes** | Baking time: **6 minutes per pan** | 30 sandwich cookies

Cookie

1 cup firmly packed brown sugar

½ cup LAND O LAKES® Butter, softened

1 egg

2¼ cups all-purpose flour

1 cup milk

⅓ cup unsweetened cocoa

1 teaspoon baking powder

½ teaspoon baking soda

½ teaspoon salt

Filling

1 (12-ounce) can soft whipped white frosting

Multi-colored decorator nonpareils

• Heat oven to 350°F. Combine brown sugar, butter and egg in large bowl. Beat at medium speed, scraping bowl often, until creamy. Reduce speed to low; add all remaining cookie ingredients. Beat until well mixed.

• Drop by tablespoonfuls onto ungreased cookie sheets; spread, using back of spoon, into 1½-inch circles. Bake for 6 to 8 minutes or until cookies are puffed and set. Cool completely.

• For each sandwich cookie, spread about 2 tablespoons frosting onto bottom-side of 1 cookie; top with second cookie, bottom-side down. Squeeze together gently. Repeat with remaining cookies and filling. Immediately roll edges of filling in decorator nonpareils.

German Chocolate Sandwich Cookies

Preparation time: **45 minutes** | Baking time: **9 minutes per pan** | **3 dozen sandwich cookies**

Filling
⅔ cup sugar
¼ cup LAND O LAKES® Butter
1 (5-ounce) can evaporated milk
1 egg, slightly beaten
1⅓ cups sweetened flaked coconut
¾ cup finely chopped pecans

Cookie
1½ cups sugar
¾ cup LAND O LAKES® Butter, softened
¼ cup milk
2 eggs
1½ teaspoons vanilla
1¾ cups all-purpose flour
¾ cup unsweetened cocoa
1 teaspoon baking soda

• Combine all filling ingredients except coconut and pecans in 2-quart saucepan. Cook over medium heat, stirring occasionally, until mixture comes to a boil and thickens (8 to 10 minutes). Stir in coconut and pecans. Cover; refrigerate at least 1 hour.

• Heat oven to 350°F. Combine 1½ cups sugar and ¾ cup butter in large bowl. Beat at medium speed, scraping bowl often, until creamy. Add milk, 2 eggs and vanilla; continue beating until well mixed. Reduce speed to low; add flour, cocoa and baking soda. Beat until well mixed.

• Drop dough by rounded teaspoonfuls, 2 inches apart, onto ungreased cookie sheets. Bake for 9 to 11 minutes or until top springs back lightly when touched. Cool completely.

• Spread 1 level tablespoonful filling onto flat-side of 1 cookie; top with second cookie, flat-side down. Squeeze together gently. Repeat with remaining cookies.

tip:
Make cookies and filling ahead and assemble just before serving.

Chocolate Glazed Mocha Wedges

Preparation time: **20 minutes** | Baking time: **23 minutes** | **16 wedges**

Bar

⅔ cup LAND O LAKES® Butter, softened

½ cup firmly packed brown sugar

2 (1-ounce) squares semi-sweet baking chocolate, melted

1 teaspoon instant espresso powder*

1¼ cups all-purpose flour

Drizzle

3 (1-ounce) squares semi-sweet baking chocolate

1 teaspoon shortening

• Heat oven to 350°F. Combine butter and brown sugar in large bowl. Beat at medium speed, scraping bowl often, until creamy. Add 2 ounces melted chocolate and espresso powder; continue beating until well mixed. Reduce speed to low; add flour. Beat until well mixed.

• Pat mixture evenly into ungreased 9-inch tart pan with removable bottom. Bake for 23 to 25 minutes or until set. Cool 10 minutes. Remove sides of tart pan. Cool completely. Cut into wedges.

• Melt 3 ounces chocolate and shortening in 1-quart saucepan over low heat, stirring occasionally, until smooth (2 to 4 minutes). Drizzle over cooled wedges. Let stand 10 minutes to set.

*Substitute instant coffee granules.

tip:

Substitute an 8- or 9-inch square baking pan for the 9-inch tart pan. Line pan with aluminum foil, extending foil over edges. Bake for 23 to 25 minutes or until set. Cool 10 minutes. Lift bars out of pan using foil. Cut into bars; drizzle with glaze as directed.

Chocolate Peanut Butter Shortbread

Preparation time: **30 minutes** | Baking time: **12 minutes** | **5 dozen cookies**

Shortbread
- ¾ cup LAND O LAKES® Butter, softened
- ⅓ cup creamy peanut butter
- ⅔ cup sugar
- 1 teaspoon vanilla
- 2 cups all-purpose flour
- ⅔ cup mini real semi-sweet chocolate chips

Coating
- 1⅓ cups mini real semi-sweet chocolate chips
- 2 tablespoons vegetable oil

• Heat oven to 375°F. Combine butter, peanut butter, sugar and vanilla in large bowl. Beat at medium speed, scraping bowl often, until creamy. Reduce speed to low; add flour. Beat just until mixture forms a dough. Stir in ⅔ cup mini chocolate chips. Pat dough evenly into lightly greased 15×10×1-inch jelly-roll pan.

• Bake for 12 to 15 minutes or until set and lightly browned. Immediately cut shortbread crosswise into 6 equal pieces; then cut 10 rows lengthwise. Cool completely. Remove from pan.

• Place all coating ingredients in small microwave-safe bowl. Microwave on HIGH until almost melted (30 seconds to 1 minute). Stir until smooth. Dip one end of each cookie stick into melted chocolate; place onto wire rack over waxed paper. Let stand until chocolate is firm (1 hour).

tip:
Use spatula to help spread dough evenly into pan.

make mine chocolate

Chocolate Mocha Brandy Dreams
Preparation time: **20 minutes** | Baking time: **6 minutes per pan** | **4 dozen cookies**

Cookie
¾ cup sugar
¾ cup LAND O LAKES® Butter, softened
1 egg
1 teaspoon vanilla
1⅔ cups all-purpose flour
⅓ cup unsweetened cocoa

Frosting
4 teaspoons LAND O LAKES™ Fat Free Half & Half or milk
1 teaspoon instant coffee granules, if desired
1 cup powdered sugar
¼ cup LAND O LAKES® Butter, softened
1 tablespoon unsweetened cocoa
1 teaspoon brandy*

Colored decorator sugar, if desired

• Combine ¾ cup sugar and ¾ cup butter in large bowl. Beat at medium speed, scraping bowl often, until creamy. Add egg and vanilla; continue beating until well mixed. Reduce speed to low; beat, gradually adding flour and cocoa, scraping bowl often, until well mixed.

• Divide dough into thirds. Wrap each third in plastic food wrap; refrigerate until firm (2 hours or overnight).

• Heat oven to 375°F. Shape dough with floured hands, one-third at a time (keeping remaining dough refrigerated), into 1-inch balls. Roll balls into 3-inch ropes. Place onto ungreased cookie sheets. Form into crescent shape; pinch ends and flatten middle slightly. Bake for 6 to 8 minutes or until set. (DO NOT OVERBAKE.) (Surface may crack slightly.) Cool completely.

• Combine half & half and coffee granules in small bowl; let stand 2 minutes. Stir until coffee granules dissolve. Add all remaining frosting ingredients. Beat at low speed, scraping bowl often, until smooth. Frost cooled cookies. Sprinkle with decorator sugar, if desired.

*Substitute ¼ teaspoon brandy extract.

tip:
To maximize space on the cookie sheet, place each crescent in the same direction.

Chocolate Chocolate Chip Cookies

Preparation time: **20 minutes** | Baking time: **12 minutes per pan** | **4 dozen cookies**

1½	cups sugar
1	cup LAND O LAKES® Butter, softened
2	eggs
2½	(1-ounce) squares unsweetened baking chocolate, melted
2	teaspoons vanilla
1½	cups all-purpose flour
2	teaspoons baking powder
½	teaspoon salt
3	cups uncooked quick-cooking oats
1	cup real semi-sweet chocolate chips

• Heat oven to 350°F. Combine sugar and butter in large bowl. Beat at medium speed, scraping bowl often, until creamy. Add eggs, chocolate and vanilla; continue beating, scraping bowl often, until well mixed. Reduce speed to low; add flour, baking powder and salt. Beat until well mixed. Stir in oats and chocolate chips.

• Drop dough by rounded tablespoonfuls, 2 inches apart, onto ungreased cookie sheets. Bake for 12 to 15 minutes or until set. (DO NOT OVERBAKE.)

Cocoa Macadamia Nut Sandies

Preparation time: **35 minutes** | Baking time: **18 minutes per pan** | **5 dozen cookies**

- 1 cup LAND O LAKES® Butter, softened
- ½ cup sugar
- ¼ cup unsweetened cocoa
- 1 tablespoon water
- 2 teaspoons vanilla
- 2 cups all-purpose flour
- 1 (3.25 ounce) jar (⅔ cup) macadamia nuts, finely chopped

- ¾ cup powdered sugar

• Heat oven to 325°F. Combine butter and sugar in large bowl. Beat at medium speed, scraping bowl often, until well mixed. Add cocoa, water and vanilla; continue beating until well mixed. Reduce speed to low; add flour. Beat until well mixed. Stir in macadamia nuts.

• Shape dough into 1-inch balls. Place 1 inch apart onto ungreased cookie sheets. Bake for 18 to 20 minutes or until set. Remove from cookie sheets. Cool completely. Roll in powdered sugar.

tip:
Want a little variety? Substitute finely chopped blanched hazelnuts or walnuts for the macadamia nuts. Still need more options? Add ¼ teaspoon almond extract or coconut flavoring along with the vanilla.

METRIC CONVERSION CHART

VOLUME MEASUREMENTS (dry)

$1/8$ teaspoon = 0.5 mL
$1/4$ teaspoon = 1 mL
$1/2$ teaspoon = 2 mL
$3/4$ teaspoon = 4 mL
1 teaspoon = 5 mL
1 tablespoon = 15 mL
2 tablespoons = 30 mL
$1/4$ cup = 60 mL
$1/3$ cup = 75 mL
$1/2$ cup = 125 mL
$2/3$ cup = 150 mL
$3/4$ cup = 175 mL
1 cup = 250 mL
2 cups = 1 pint = 500 mL
3 cups = 750 mL
4 cups = 1 quart = 1 L

VOLUME MEASUREMENTS (fluid)

1 fluid ounce (2 tablespoons) = 30 mL
4 fluid ounces ($1/2$ cup) = 125 mL
8 fluid ounces (1 cup) = 250 mL
12 fluid ounces ($1\frac{1}{2}$ cups) = 375 mL
16 fluid ounces (2 cups) = 500 mL

WEIGHTS (mass)

$1/2$ ounce = 15 g
1 ounce = 30 g
3 ounces = 90 g
4 ounces = 120 g
8 ounces = 225 g
10 ounces = 285 g
12 ounces = 360 g
16 ounces = 1 pound = 450 g

DIMENSIONS

$1/16$ inch = 2 mm
$1/8$ inch = 3 mm
$1/4$ inch = 6 mm
$1/2$ inch = 1.5 cm
$3/4$ inch = 2 cm
1 inch = 2.5 cm

OVEN TEMPERATURES

250°F = 120°C
275°F = 140°C
300°F = 150°C
325°F = 160°C
350°F = 180°C
375°F = 190°C
400°F = 200°C
425°F = 220°C
450°F = 230°C

BAKING PAN SIZES

Utensil	Size in Inches/Quarts	Metric Volume	Size in Centimeters
Baking or Cake Pan (square or rectangular)	$8 \times 8 \times 2$	2 L	$20 \times 20 \times 5$
	$9 \times 9 \times 2$	2.5 L	$23 \times 23 \times 5$
	$12 \times 8 \times 2$	3 L	$30 \times 20 \times 5$
	$13 \times 9 \times 2$	3.5 L	$33 \times 23 \times 5$
Loaf Pan	$8 \times 4 \times 3$	1.5 L	$20 \times 10 \times 7$
	$9 \times 5 \times 3$	2 L	$23 \times 13 \times 7$
Round Layer Cake Pan	$8 \times 1\frac{1}{2}$	1.2 L	20×4
	$9 \times 1\frac{1}{2}$	1.5 L	23×4
Pie Plate	$8 \times 1\frac{1}{4}$	750 mL	20×3
	$9 \times 1\frac{1}{4}$	1 L	23×3
Baking Dish or Casserole	1 quart	1 L	—
	$1\frac{1}{2}$ quart	1.5 L	—
	2 quart	2 L	—